Tribute to the Deltics

Tom Heavyside

DAVID & CHARLES

Newton Abbot   London   North Pomfret (Vt)

Contents

British Library Cataloguing in Publication Data

Heavyside, Tom
    Tribute to the Deltics.
    1. Diesel locomotives – Great Britain
    I. Title
    625.2'662'0941   TJ619

    ISBN 978-14463-0584-3

Photoset by
Northern Phototypesetting Co, Bolton
and printed in Great Britain
by Biddles Ltd, Guildford, Surrey
for David & Charles (Publishers) Limited
Brunel House, Newton Abbot, Devon

Published in the United States of America
by David & Charles Inc
North Pomfret, Vermont 05053, USA

Introduction

Introduced during the modernisation of the railway system the last surviving members of the 3300hp diesel-electric Deltic class locomotives were, at the time of writing, in their twenty first year of service on the Eastern and Scottish Regions of British Rail – an appropriate time to pay tribute to an outstanding batch of locomotives which have endeared themselves to the hearts of railwaymen and enthusiasts alike, despite the fact that initially they displaced 55 of the beloved Gresley, Thompson, and Peppercorn Pacifics on East Coast main line duties.

The story really begins late in 1955 when English Electric released on loan to BR a Co-Co locomotive which, at the time, was revolutionary. This was the prototype Deltic design which utilised two Napier 18-cylinder opposed piston engines rated at 1650hp (derated marine engines), the resultant 3300hp making it at that time the most powerful diesel locomotive in the world, while at 106 tons it was also a comparative lightweight design. The locomotive went first to the London Midland Region where it was put through its paces on various trials and ordinary service trains. Its performance, to say the least, was impressive, and some of the BR hierarchy, particularly on the Eastern Region, were taking note.

By spring 1958 BR with strong pushing from the ER had decided to purchase 22 3300hp 100mph Deltic locomotives to improve journey times on the East Coast route between London and Edinburgh pending electrification – an event still awaited except for suburban services from Kings Cross! In January 1961 the first of the production order emerged from English Electric's Vulcan Works at Newton-le-Willows, Lancashire, finished in a two tone green livery with white cab surrounds and numbered D9001 (No D9000 was delivered second), the remainder following over the next 15 months. Compared with the prototype some detail differences were incorporated, including a slimmer outline and tumblehome at the bottom of the sides, and a reduced weight of 99 tons, giving them a very wide route availability. BR also agreed with English Electric that EE should maintain the class; as a mark of the faith the latter had in its product, a penalty clause was written into the contract to the effect that if certain annual mileages were not achieved then the payments due would be reduced accordingly. This arrangement lasted for eight years.

At the planning stage it was realised that if maximum benefit was to be obtained from what were expensive machines then the time spent at depots and in works had to be kept to an absolute minimum. Thus a repair by replacement programme was introduced whereby even main components such as bogies, generators, and engines were held as spares, so that whenever a part required attention it was simply substituted, enabling the locomotive to return to traffic while the disabled item was overhauled pending further use. In practice this worked well, and Doncaster Works for example could exchange an engine in a single eight hour shift.

Following acceptance trials the Deltics were allocated to one of three depots, Finsbury Park and Haymarket each receiving eight and Gateshead six; once over some early teething troubles they soon began to live up to expectation. With the timetable introduced in June 1962 their capabilities for rapid acceleration and steady 100mph running began to be exploited, six trains

No 55013 *The Black Watch* coasts towards Gilberdyke Junction with the 12.34 Hull–Kings Cross on 30 May 1981.

between London and Edinburgh being scheduled to make the journey in 6hr, an improvement of over 1hr for The Flying Scotsman against its previous steam timing, while the up Tees-Tyne Pullman was allowed but 35min for the 44.1 miles between Darlington and York, an average of 75.6mph, then the fastest start to stop average speed ever seen on BR.

Apart from some very short lived variations, the 55s, as they were later to become known under their BR TOPS classification, remained at their original depots until 1979. During this time they were mostly used on intensive diagrams covering fast expresses and overnight trains between Kings Cross, Newcastle and Edinburgh, and the West Riding. At times they were used on duties which took them to such other places as Cleethorpes and Hull, but when straying from their main routes it was usually due to engineering work or mishap necessitating a detour to by-pass a closed section of line. In the early years Deltic performance was somewhat hampered by permanent way limitations but with a steady programme of trackwork during the 1970s to increase the line speed at many locations, combined with the introduction of colour-light signalling throughout, the northern cities were gradually brought closer to Kings Cross! For instance by 1973 the time for the 392.7 miles between London and the Scottish capital had been reduced to 5½hr, while Leeds, 186.2 miles from Kings Cross could be reached in 2hr 28min.

Rightly it was decided that such prestigious locomotives as the Deltics should be named, and first off the mark was the Eastern Region which followed an old LNER tradition by affixing without formality, soon after entry into service, names of famous racehorses, all except one being past winners of at least one of the five English Classics; Alycidon could manage but second place in the 1948 St Leger! The Scottish and the then North Eastern Region chose regimental names, which appeared from June 1962, the majority unveiled with due ceremony, and with full military colours in evidence. The last was not named until 11 September 1965 when No D9019 was christened Royal Highland Fusilier at Glasgow Central. Some of these names had previously been used on steam locomotives, and not all on former LNER types.

Over the years various modifications have been made to the fleet, including the fitting of air brakes and electric train heating equipment to allow haulage of Mk 2 coaching stock. Externally the most noticeable alterations were first the addition of yellow warning panels at each end and from 1966 repainting in standard rail blue following a change of BR policy, while marker lights replaced the train indicator blinds during the mid-1970s. Renumbering into the series 55001–22 was carried out between October 1973 and May 1974.

In the last century and a half man has continually been looking for more rapid modes of travel, a dominant reason for the birth of the Deltics, but which in turn has now seen them ousted from the head of the fastest trains along the East Coast main line. The beginning of the end came in September 1977 when crew training commenced on Inter-City 125 High Speed Trains and from March 1978 IC125 units gradually began to take over the daytime Deltic diagrams. The recast May 1979 timetable saw the IC125s in command although initially their full impact on the longer journeys to Scotland was marred by the Penmanshiel Tunnel collapse in the previous March which effectively closed the line between Berwick and Dunbar until the following August.

However for Deltic admirers the period since May 1979 has been full of interest, starting with the transfer of the Gateshead and Haymarket locomotives to York that same month. While they retained a few turns between London and Edinburgh including the overnight sleepers, they were then diagrammed to semi-fast expresses between Kings Cross and York, connecting with IC125s on longer journeys, and to trains between the capital and Hull, one being The Hull Executive, scheduled on the down run to cover the 138.6 miles to Retford in 91min. Frequently they have powered Kings Cross–Cleethorpes trains, stopping trains between Newcastle and Edinburgh and, even more notable, at times became almost regular visitors to Liverpool Lime Street with services from York and Newcastle. The important Plymouth–Edinburgh service also became a Deltic working between York and Edinburgh. North of the Border their lay-over periods at Edinburgh between night duties has on occasions been utilised on trains to Aberdeen and elsewhere while employment on empty stock duties between Edinburgh Waverley and Craigentinny carriage sidings is not unknown. Not surprisingly they have also been much in demand for enthusiasts specials.

Finsbury Park depot long held the Deltics in esteem, which manifested itself in April 1979 when No 55003 Meld was adorned with white cab surrounds, and subsequently the rest of its active allocation was treated similarly, this refinement,

The English Electric prototype Deltic ran some 450,000 miles on British Rail between October 1955 and March 1961 before being retired by the makers, who subsequently presented it to the Science Museum, South Kensington, London, where it is viewed in the transport gallery. (*Crown Copyright. Science Museum, London*)

coupled with the generally high standard of cleanliness making Finsbury Park Deltics readily distinguishable at a distance. York responded by painting the city coat of arms above the numbers on its locomotives. In June 1981 Finsbury Park's Deltics joined the rest of the fleet at York and regrettably at the same time their white cab surrounds gave way to standard blue again.

It is sad that at the time of writing the major part of this book the 55s were in their last days on BR, some withdrawals from stock already having taken place, the first being Nos 55001 *St Paddy* and 55020 *Nimbus* in January 1980, although by then both had been inactive for over 20 months. At the end of August 1981 four more had been earmarked for the breaker's hammer and by January 1982 all the remainder had retired from active service. Meanwhile a number of farewell specials, some to previously untravelled parts of BR, were undertaken so that enthusiasts in parts of the country not on regular Deltic routes had a chance to see them in action. Deltic activity under BR ownership came to an end on 2 January 1982 with a special from Kings Cross to Edinburgh and back, No 55015 *Tulyar* hauling the train north, and No 55022 *Royal Scots Grey* doing the honours on the return run. Thousands lined the East Coast main line to pay homage while millions witnessed some of the scenes on television news bulletins. It was a fitting finale for a much admired class of locomotives.

Fortunately not all will be consigned to the scrapyard for, like the prototype, examples are destined for preservation. No 55002 *The King's Own Yorkshire Light Infantry* had already been reserved by the National Railway Museum, York (housed next door to its present shed) and since December 1980 had been running in two-tone green livery again, complete with former BR emblem, by courtesy of the Friends of the National Railway Museum. The Deltic Preservation Society was expected to purchase one and others are considering doing likewise.

Even so with the distinctive throb of the Deltics now silent on BR and as their stately profiles no longer haunt such places as Newcastle, Newark, and Northallerton, their passing will be mourned by many. They have served the railways well, no

locomotives having previously been worked so hard or intensively – some recording over three million miles in revenue earning service, and deservedly they will take their place in history alongside the steam giants of the past. A full technical and historical survey of the class can be found in the late Brian Webb's *Deltic Locomotives of British Rail* published by David & Charles, while this volume comprises a pictorial tribute to their work during the last ten years, both along well trodden routes and in places where they were eminent visitors. I hope the following pages will serve as a reminder of those great days when the Deltics were indeed Kings of the (East Coast) Iron Road.

Acknowledgements

I would like to express my gratitude for help received in various ways while compiling this book to Allan Baker, Murray Brown, Derek Mercer, Christina Siviter, and the Public Relations Officer, British Rail, York. Also to my fellow photographers who assisted with material away from the East Coast main line, their prints being acknowledged individually, while the remainder are from my own camera. As usual Marlene McPherson has done sterling work on the typewriter.

Bolton, Lancs.   Tom Heavyside
September 1981

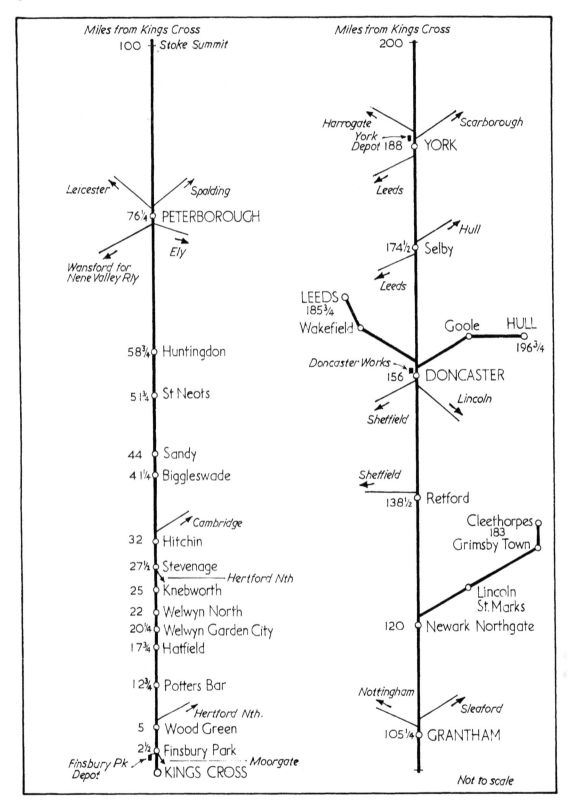

Miles from Kings Cross

100 ┼ Stoke Summit

Leicester / *Spalding*

76¼ PETERBOROUGH

Ely

Wansford for Nene Valley Rly

58¾ Huntingdon

51¾ St Neots

44 Sandy

41¼ Biggleswade

Cambridge

32 Hitchin

27½ Stevenage — *Hertford Nth*

25 Knebworth

22 Welwyn North

20¼ Welwyn Garden City

17¾ Hatfield

12¾ Potters Bar

Hertford Nth.

5 Wood Green

2½ Finsbury Park — *Moorgate*

Finsbury Pk. Depot

KINGS CROSS

Miles from Kings Cross

200 ┬

Harrogate — *Scarborough*

York Depot 188 — YORK

Leeds

174½ Selby — *Hull*

Leeds

LEEDS 185¾

Wakefield

Goole HULL

196¾

Doncaster Works

156 DONCASTER

Lincoln

Sheffield

Sheffield

138½ Retford

Cleethorpes 183

Grimsby Town

Lincoln St. Marks

120 Newark Northgate

Nottingham / *Sleaford*

105¼ GRANTHAM

Not to scale

Principal Deltic routes. Mileages are shown from Kings Cross. Only passenger lines are shown and not all London suburban stations are included.

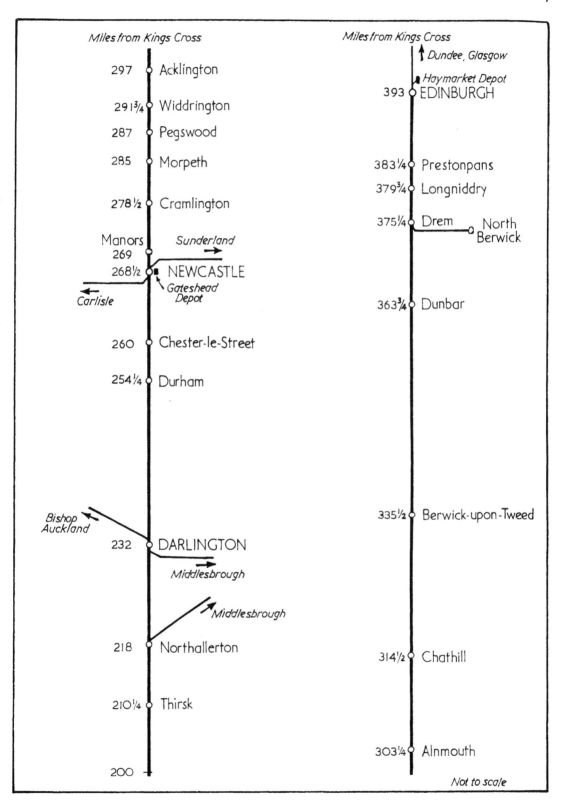

Classic production series Deltic profile – No 55016 *Gordon Highlander* outside Haymarket shed, Edinburgh, on 26 May 1974.

ALONG THE EAST COAST ROUTE

Left: A familiar sight at Kings Cross for over two decades – a Deltic at the head of a northbound express. Here No 55014 *The Duke of Wellington's Regiment* waits for the guard's green flag with the 19.35 to Hull on 7 July 1980.

Bottom left: No 55016 *Gordon Highlander* accelerates through the London suburbs at Finsbury Park with the 18.05 Kings Cross–York on 8 May 1981, while on the right No 55015 *Tulyar*, together with Class 47s Nos 47210 and 47185 await their next duties in Finsbury Park depot yard. The small plaque between the marker lights on *Tulyar* commemorates the locomotive's participation in the Rocket 150 celebrations at Rainhill in May 1980 (see page 44).

Below: No 55021 *Argyll & Sutherland Highlander* emerges from Welwyn South Tunnel with a train for Kings Cross on 4 September 1978.

Above: With a morning express from Kings Cross No 55011 *The Royal Northumberland Fusiliers* passes Hitchin Permanent Way Yard on 5 September 1978. At the moment Hitchin is as far as the overhead catenary extends along the East Coast main line, electric trains from Kings Cross for Royston branching off just north of the station at Cambridge Junction.

Below: A Deltic on a double-headed train is a rarity, but on 9 May 1981 No 55007 *Pinza*, due to an electrical fault, is piloted by Class 40 No 40006 past Offord Cluny, just south of Huntingdon, with the 9.33 Hull–Kings Cross.

Right: Later that day at the 1977 rebuilt Huntingdon station heads turn to view the arrival of No 55019 *Royal Highland Fusilier* with the 14.05 from Kings Cross to York.

Top left: Glimpsed over a fence at Abbots Ripton, between Huntingdon and Peterborough, No 55022 *Royal Scots Grey* hurries by with the 10.05 Kings Cross to York on 5 May 1981. This was the first of the former Scottish Region Deltics to be named – on 18 June 1962 at Edinburgh, the name having previously been carried by LMS Royal Scot class 4-6-0 No 46101.

Left: Earlier the same day No 55012 *Crepello*, on one of its last duties before withdrawal later that month, hauling the 8.05 Kings Cross–Hull, eases out of Peterborough past the locomotive stabling point occupied by Nos 37023, 40092 and 31292. *Crepello* was the name of the 1957 Derby winner.

Above: Royal Scots Grey, again with the 10.05 from Kings Cross, although extended to Edinburgh for the summer months, rushes towards the entrance to Peascliffe Tunnel, north of Grantham, on Saturday 23 August 1980. Scheduled to arrive in Edinburgh at 16.21 the train will be overtaken by both the 10.45 (SO) and 11.00 IC125 departures from Kings Cross.

Above: In the days of semaphore signals along parts of the former Great Northern Railway main line No 55017 *The Durham Light Infantry* races through Newark Northgate in charge of a down express on 9 October 1976. To the right a diesel multiple-unit waits to form a later connecting service to Lincoln and Cleethorpes.

Top right: Prior to renumbering No 9020 *Nimbus* nears Retford with a northbound train on 16 June 1973. Bearing the name of the 1949 Derby winner *Nimbus* was the shortest lived Deltic, entering service in February 1962 it was one of two condemned on 5 January 1980.

Right: With Doncaster Traction Maintenance Depot to be seen in the top left hand corner, No 55008 *The Green Howards* approaches Bridge Junction with a train destined for Scotland from London on 14 August 1976. LMS Royal Scot 4-6-0 No 46133 carried the same name.

Above: The down Flying Scotsman speeds along the centre down fast line at Doncaster behind No 55005 *The Prince of Wales's Own Regiment of Yorkshire* on 14 August 1976. In the background is Doncaster Works, 'The Plant', visited frequently by the Deltics over the years for change of engines, bogies etc, and other heavy maintenance work.

Below: Having entered one time North Eastern Railway territory at Shaftholme Junction, just north of Doncaster, No 9010 *The King's Own Scottish Borderer* passes Henwick Hall level crossing, two miles south of Selby, while bound for Scotland on 30 June 1973. Soon this section of line will no longer form part of the East Coast main line, as in order to avoid future subsidence problems from the new Selby coalfield a new high speed diversionary route is under construction from Temple Hirst, $4\frac{1}{2}$ miles south of Selby, to Colton, on the Leeds to York line.

Right: Peeping out from York station's magnificent arched roof, behind which can be seen the Royal Station Hotel, Gateshead allocated No 55011 *The Royal Northumberland Fusiliers* waits to depart north with the Sunday 13.00 Kings Cross–Edinburgh on 7 September 1975.

Above: At Darlington passengers can view another fine overall roof (by-passed on the east side by non-stopping trains) and on 26 August 1978 the driver of Finsbury Park's No 55009 *Alycidon* looks for the right away signal from platform 4 heading the 9.00 from London to the Scottish capital.

Below: Shortly after leaving Durham, Haymarket-based No 55016 *Gordon Highlander* makes for London at Sunderland Bridge on 3 September 1977. No 55016 was named at Aberdeen on 28 July 1964 and during the ceremony another *Gordon Highlander*, preserved Great North of Scotland Railway 4-4-0 No 49 (BR No 62277), stood at its side. The name was also bestowed on LMS Royal Scot class No 46106.

Right: In 1955 the racehorse *Meld* won three of the five English Classics, the 1,000 Guineas, the Oaks and the St Leger. It was thus a very appropriate name to adorn No 55003, here stopped on the northern end of Durham viaduct with the up Talisman while business is transacted at the station on 3 September 1977. As they cross the viaduct passengers will be able to enjoy a splendid view of the city with the castle and cathedral dominating the scene to the east.

Above: Having just left Newcastle (visible in the background) with the 10.20 to London, No 55011 *The Royal Northumberland Fusiliers* comes off the King Edward Bridge at Gateshead on 28 August 1978. On the right is Gateshead shed, while behind the train another Tyne bridge, for the Tyne & Wear Metro, can be seen under construction.

Below: A humble duty for a Deltic! No 55022 *Royal Scots Grey* arrives at Newcastle with five coaches forming the 14.25 stopping service from Edinburgh, to return north later with the 17.35 all stations to Dunbar then Edinburgh train on 7 March 1980. The 55s have been used frequently on such trains since their demise from the principal daytime services.

Right: The clock indicates what should be a right time arrival in Newcastle for No 55004 *Queen's Own Highlander* passing Manors with the 9.50 Edinburgh–Plymouth on 23 April 1980. No 55004 hauled the train as far as York, and would then travel back from there on the 7.22 Plymouth–Edinburgh, one of the few daytime Deltic diagrams north of York after the introduction of Inter-City 125 units.

Top left: Before the days of white cab surrounds on the Finsbury Park Deltics No 55007 *Pinza* curves into Alnmouth with the up Aberdonian, the 10.30 Aberdeen–Kings Cross, which it took over at Edinburgh on 14 June 1976.

Left: No 55015 *Tulyar* passes the goods loops at Grantshouse while returning to Edinburgh with the 7.22 from Plymouth on 16 April 1981. Notice the white cab surrounds which marked the Finsbury Park allocation from their York counterparts at this time.

Above: From Berwick, East Coast main line trains follow ex-North British Railway metals and amidst beautiful countryside at Horn Burn, between Reston and Ayton, No 55010 *The King's Own Scottish Borderer* (minus nameplate) heads south on 16 April 1981 with an Easter holiday Edinburgh–Kings Cross extra. On 16 January 1973 No 55010 became the first diesel locomotive to clock two million miles on BR – achieved in $11\frac{1}{2}$ years.

Overleaf: Riding high above the Tweed on the Royal Border Bridge, No 55013 *The Black Watch* powers the 9.50 Edinburgh–Plymouth away from Berwick station, which stands on the site of the Great Hall of Berwick Castle, on 17 April 1981. Not since 1482 has the Tweed at this point formed the border between England and Scotland, trains crossing into Scotland three miles north of Berwick at Marshall Meadows. The LMS also designated an engine in honour of The Black Watch regiment – Royal Scot class No 46102.

Top left: No 55001 *St Paddy* displays the attributes of its namesake (winner of the 1960 Derby and St Leger) at Grantshouse en route between the capitals with the 13.00 from Kings Cross on 17 June 1976. While the first to be delivered *St Paddy* was also one of the first to be withdrawn, along with *Nimbus*, on 5 January 1980.

Left: Prestonpans was not controlled by the Edinburgh power signalbox when this photograph was taken on 16 June 1976 of the down Flying Scotsman nearing journey's end behind No 55009 *Alycidon*. As well as the semaphore signals notice too the sausage type station sign mounted on a modern lamp standard!

Above: The twin Napier engines of No 55018 *Ballymoss* send a vapour trail over Edinburgh as it storms away with an Easter Monday extra to Kings Cross on 20 April 1981. In the station, situated between the old (on the left) and new parts of Edinburgh can be seen representatives of Classes 08 and 47 together with an ICI 125 unit.

IN THE WEST RIDING

Above: From their inception until they succumbed to Inter-City 125s the Deltics had regular diagrams to the West Riding (now West Yorkshire), first into the now closed Leeds Central station and then to the modern Leeds City, with some turns taking them also to Bradford or Harrogate. On occasions since May 1979 they have proved able runners while deputising for IC125s and on one such duty No 55010 *The King's Own Scottish Borderer* stands ready to leave Bradford Exchange with the Sunday 16.15 to Kings Cross on 8 July 1979. The tower of Bradford cathedral can be seen above the locomotive. (*Gavin Morrison*)

Above: At a time when train indicator blinds were still in use, two young spotters look approvingly at No 55006 *The Fife & Forfar Yeomanry* as it glints in the evening sunshine preparing to leave Leeds City with train No 1A35, the 18.25 to London on 27 April 1974.

Below: Leaving the environs of Leeds city centre behind, No 55012 *Crepello* takes the empty stock of a service from London to Neville Hill carriage sidings on the murky afternoon of 11 November 1978.

Above: On a glorious summer's evening the Sunday 17.50 Leeds–Kings Cross in the care of No 55011 *The Royal Northumberland Fusiliers* passes Lofthouse Colliery, Outwood, north of Wakefield, on 9 July 1978.

ON HUMBERSIDE SERVICES

Top right: The Deltics were no strangers to both North and South Humberside, particularly in recent years, and on 26 July 1980 the first of Finsbury Park's allocation to receive white cab surrounds, No 55003 *Meld*, is framed by the station roof at Hull before departure with the 12.34 to Kings Cross.

Right: South of the Humber No 55006 *The Fife & Forfar Yeomanry* rolls into Barnetby with a Kings Cross–Cleethorpes working on 27 July 1979.

Top left: The signalman at Gilberdyke Junction follows the progress of No 55013 *The Black Watch* coming off the Doncaster line with the 8.05 Kings Cross—Hull on 30 May 1981. The line straight ahead leads to Selby and Leeds.

Left: Later the same day No 55016 *Gordon Highlander* drifts into Goole at the head of the 12.05 from Kings Cross to Hull. From the following Monday the two trains illustrated on the left hand page, and the corresponding return workings, were diagrammed to be covered by HC125s.

Above: Rain had set in as No 55021 *Argyll & Sutherland Highlander* left Cleethorpes with the stock off the 13.05 Kings Cross—Cleethorpes forming the 17.46 to London, here drawing to a halt at Grimsby Town on 28 July 1979.

Above: On 8 May 1981 No 55007 *Pinza* sojourns outside Finsbury Park depot.

Top right: In May 1979 York became only the fourth depot to have Deltics on its books; on 28 April 1981 No 5501 *The Black Watch* awaits attention inside the maintenance depot in company with Class 31 No 31319 on the left and Class 47 No 47528.

Right: David and Goliath inside Gateshead depot! One of BR's smallest locomotives Class 03 shunter No 215 (since withdrawn) is somewhat dwarfed by No 9011 *The Royal Northumberland Fusiliers* on 28 August 1972.

ON SHED

Above: No 55010 *The King's Own Scottish Borderer* straddles the inspection pits at Haymarket depot, Edinburgh, the only Scottish Region shed to have had responsibility for the Deltics, on 21 May 1978.

OFF THE BEATEN TRACK

Top right: On occasions Deltics have been diverted of their normal runs for one reason or another and here, since the regular route was closed because of work in connection with the new Doncaster power signalbox, No 55018 *Ballymoss* rides former Great Central Railway tracks through Woodhouse, near Sheffield, with the Sunday 8.30 Hull–Kings Cross. The East Coast main line was regained at Retford. (*Les Nixon*)

Right: On 13 July 1976 No 55017 *The Durham Light Infantry* traverses the nominally freight only section between Walton and Crofton West Junctions, near Wakefield, with a Leeds–Kings Cross train, travelling from Wakefield to Doncaster via Knottingley instead of the usual way through South Elmsall. The same North East based regiment also gave its name to LNER V2 class 2-6-2 No 60964.

Above: Surprise visitor to Blackpool North with an excursion from Castleford, No 55003 *Meld* commences the journey back to Yorkshire from the Lancashire seaside resort, while on the right, overlooked by the famous Blackpool Tower, a Class 45 waits for the road with another special, on 7 September 1980. (*Peter Fitton*)

Right: Liverpool Lime Street plays host to No 55018 *Ballymoss*, here ready to return to home pastures with the 16.05 to Newcastle on 8 September 1979. *Ballymoss* had arrived earlier with the 9.28 from Newcastle. (*Gavin Morrison*)

SPECIAL DUTIES

The Deltics popularity has meant many requests to BR for their use on enthusiasts specials (some taking them into very unfamiliar territory), No 55002 *The King's Own Yorkshire Light Infantry* being one of the favourites following its emergence from Doncaster Works in two-tone green livery in December 1980. On 4 May 1981 No 55002 broke new ground when it powered the BR sponsored Deltic Fenman tour from Finsbury Park via Bishop's Stortford, Cambridge, and Spalding, to the privately-operated Nene Valley Railway, near Peterborough, and at its destination, with virtually every vantage point taken, it is signalled to a halt at Wansford. It is seen *bottom left* with strange companions, on the right former Swedish State Railways Class S 2-6-2T No 1178 and, at the far end of the station, BR standard Class 5 4-6-0 No 73050 *City of Peterborough*.

During the afternoon *The King's Own Yorkshire Light Infantry* headed a rake of continental coaching stock including Wagons Lits sleeping and dining cars *left*, into Orton Mere from Wansford, forming a Nene Valley Railway internal service, an honour indeed on a line where steam normally reigns supreme on passenger trains!

Below: Destination Lowestoft: No 55015 *Tulyar* sprints through Letchworth, England's first garden city, with a special from Kings Cross on 3 September 1978. The train had left the East Coast main line at Cambridge Junction, Hitchin.

Above: Watched by an admiring audience on the end of the former Furness Railway down platform at Carnforth No 55003 *Meld* removes the empty stock of its BR Sheffield Merrymaker rail enthusiasts excursion to the sidings south of the station, adjacent to the electrified West Coast main line, on 23 July 1978. *Meld* then travelled light over Shap to Carlisle, while its train, after passengers had had time to sample the delights of Steamtown, followed later behind the now withdrawn electric locomotive No 84003.

Top right: Later that day, having taken over from No 84003 at the Border City, *Meld* heads the special towards Ribblehead viaduct on the Carlisle—Sheffield section of the tour. Above the first coach can be seen the lonely Blea Moor signalbox.

Right: Having started at Manchester Victoria with a T&N Railtours circular trip to Carlisle, Newcastle, and York, No 55022 *Royal Scots Grey* prepares to stop at Bolton before continuing its northbound run to Carlisle via Euxton Junction and the West Coast main line on 7 October 1979.

Above: After watching a great pageant of steam locomotives at the Rocket 150 celebrations at Rainhill on 24 May 1980, spectators turned their attention to more modern forms of motive power, which rightly included a representative of the Deltic class. Gliding sedately past the main stands a resplendent No 55015 *Tulyar* has two electric locomotives in tow – Class 86 No 86214 *Sans Pareil* and preserved Class 76 No 26020.

Top right: On a few occasions Deltics have graced Western Region metals, and on 19 February 1978 No 55018 *Ballymoss* was rostered for a Railway Pictorial Publications railtour from Paddington to Paignton, but due to adverse weather conditions in which the West Country was snowed up, got no further than Bristol. *Ballymoss* is pictured under the overall roof at snow-covered Bristol Temple Meads before its early departure back to London. The excursion was re-run two weeks later with No 55003 *Meld* in charge. (*Graham Scott-Lowe*)

The last rites – 2 January 1982. In dismal weather conditions but with an air of triumph, No 55022 *Royal Scots Grey* sets out from Edinburgh Waverley (displaying an exhaust that would do justice to any steam locomotive) with the last Deltic passenger working, the return leg of the 'Deltic Scotsman Farewell' to Kings Cross – the train having come north behind No 55015 *Tulyar*. *Royal Scots Grey* also carried the headboard Farewell To Thy Greatness along with a wreath. Thousands lined the East Coast route to see the special pass while millions witnessed some of the activity during television news bulletins, a fitting finale to the Deltics' work on BR.

EAST COAST LAMENT

The Deltics will be remembered chiefly for their exploits along the East Coast main line between Kings Cross and Edinburgh, therefore it seems fitting to take a further brief look at them on a route which they almost made their own!

Left: No 55005 *The Prince of Wales's Own Regiment of Yorkshire* gets a clear road at Grantshouse with the 7.45 Kings Cross–Edinburgh on 15 June 1976.

Above: On a dull 6 March 1980 No 55015 *Tulyar* almost appears to shout defiantly at one of its successors, an Inter-City 125 forming an up train, as it leaves Newcastle with the 7.22 Plymouth–Edinburgh.

Below: End of the line for No 55003 *Meld* facing the buffer stops at Kings Cross after arriving from the north on 7 July 1980. *Meld* has already run its last, being withdrawn in December 1980, and soon the remaining Deltics will have been disposed of by BR, but one thing for sure – they'll ne'er be forgot.

ARGYLL & SUTHERLAND HIGHLANDER

Deltic Numbers, Names and Allocations

Original Number	Final Number	Name	Depot Allocation 31/12/72	31/12/79	31/8/81
D9000	55022	Royal Scots Grey	HA	YK	YK
D9001	55001	St Paddy	FP	FP	WD
D9002	55002	The King's Own Yorkshire Light Infantry	GD	YK	YK
D9003	55003	Meld	FP	FP	WD
D9004	55004	Queen's Own Highlander	HA	YK	YK
D9005	55005	The Prince of Wales's Own Regiment of Yorkshire	GD	YK	WD
D9006	55006	The Fife & Forfar Yeomanry	HA	YK	WD
D9007	55007	Pinza	FP	FP	YK
D9008	55008	The Green Howards	GD	YK	YK
D9009	55009	Alycidon	FP	FP	YK
D9010	55010	The King's Own Scottish Borderer	HA	YK	YK
D9011	55011	The Royal Northumberland Fusiliers	GD	YK	YK
D9012	55012	Crepello	FP	FP	WD
D9013	55013	The Black Watch	HA	YK	YK
D9014	55014	The Duke of Wellington's Regiment	GD	YK	YK
D9015	55015	Tulyar	FP	FP	YK
D9016	55016	Gordon Highlander	HA	YK	YK
D9017	55017	The Durham Light Infantry	GD	YK	YK
D9018	55018	Ballymoss	FP	FP	YK
D9019	55019	Royal Highland Fusilier	HA	YK	YK
D9020	55020	Nimbus	FP	FP	WD
D9021	55021	Argyll & Sutherland Highlander	HA	YK	YK

Abbreviations:

- FP   Finsbury Park
- GD   Gateshead
- HA   Haymarket
- YK   York
- WD   Withdrawn

Note: The D prefixes on the original numbers were deleted following the end of steam traction on British Rail in August 1968.

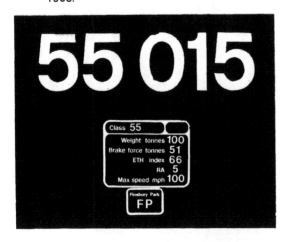

Above: The nameplate of No 55021 *Argyll & Sutherland Highlander.*

Left: Cabside details of No 55015. Towards the end of the Deltic era nameplate and number rubbing – in the manner of brass rubbings – had become a popular past-time among younger enthusiasts.